Healthy Lifestyles

EXERCISE

Katie Dicker

amicus
mankato, minnesota

Published in the United States by
Amicus
P.O. Box 1329, Mankato, Minnesota 56002

Printed in China by Midas Printing International Ltd

Library of Congress Cataloging-in-Publication Data

Dicker, Katie.
  Exercise / Katie Dicker.
     p. cm. -- (Healthy lifestyles)
  Includes index.
  ISBN 978-60753-086-2 (library binding)
  1. Physical fitness for youth. 2. Exercise for youth. I. Title.
  GV341.4.D53 2011
  613.7'043--dc22

                           200904756

Consultant: Adrian King
Editor: Sonya Newland
Designer: Graham Rich
Picture researcher: Sophie Schrey

Picture Credits
Alamy: 13t (Sportsweb), 15t (Harriet Cummings), 26 (David R. Frazier Photolibrary, Inc.), 30 (Picture Partners);
Corbis: 24 (Franck Robichon/epa), 33 (Yang Lei C/xh/Xinhua Press), 38 (Mark. E. Gibson), 39r (Justin Lane/epa);
Dreamstime: 11b (Jean-Marie Guyon), 19 (Olga Besnard), 20b (D. McCale), 22-23 (Godfer), 23t (Andres Rodriguez),
29 (Sophieso), 31b (Laurent Hamels), 32b (Mtomczak), 37 (Eastwest Imaging), 40 (Jennifer Walkz), 43 (Shariff Che'
Lah); **Fotolia:** 6 (EastWest Imaging), 7 (Monkey Business), 20t (Moodboard), 23b (Marzanna Syncerz), 28 (Iofoto);
Getty Images: 34 (David Madison); **iStock:** 8 (Indykb), 9 (Karen Struthers), 11t (Frederick Kaselow), 14 (Indykb),
15b (U Star Pix), 16t (Indykb), 17 (Timothy Large), 25t (Chris Schmidt), 27 (Diego Cervo), 32t (Dana Bartekoske), 35
(Matjaz Boncina), 36 (Alberto L. Pomares G.), 41 (Chris Schmidt), 42 (Richardson Maneze); **Science Photo Library:**
13b (Paul Rapson), 18 (NASA), 21 (Henning Dalhoff/Bonnier Publications); **Shutterstock:** 25b (Philip Lange), 31tl
(Juriah Mosin), 31tr (Juriah Mosin), 39l (Galina Barskaya).
Artwork by Graham Rich.

05 10
PO 1560

9 8 7 6 5 4 3 2 1

Contents

Introduction

When was the last time you got active? What did it feel like? Even if you think it's been a while, you've probably been moving a lot of muscles without even realizing it.

Time for Action

Every time you move and exert yourself, you're helping to keep your body in good shape. Our bodies are like cars or machines—they need to be moved regularly to keep in good condition. Some people are more active than others. They may be fitter or more naturally able. But whatever your ability, now is the time to take action for a new, more mobile you.

Why Exercise?

Apart from the fact that getting active is good for your body—helping your heart and lungs to work more efficiently, and increasing your strength and flexibility—there are other benefits to enjoy.

Exercising can be a great way to spend time with friends and family.

Exercise makes you look and feel healthy. It will tone and strengthen your muscles, improving your body shape and your posture.

DID YOU KNOW?

Exercise can improve your mood. Regular activity increases the amount of endorphins (the hormones that make you feel happy) and unlocks natural antidepressants, such as serotonin, in the brain.

If you want to lose weight, regular exercise will help you achieve your goals. It will also help cleanse your skin, and will give you a glowing vitality.

If you're prone to coughs and colds, exercise may be the answer. Regular exercise helps boost the immune system to keep common ailments at bay. Getting active is a great way to de-stress and rest your mind, and to relax tensed muscles. It's even been shown to help improve memory and brain function! And the benefits are long-lasting. Studies have shown that regular exercise when you're young helps to reduce the risk of serious diseases later in life, such as heart disease, cancer, and diabetes.

How Do I Get Active?

Exercise is easy to do and doesn't have to cost money or take a lot of time. While some people like to get involved in activities such as team sports, time at the gym, or a walking group, you probably already enjoy many things that keep you fit. Going for a brisk walk or swim, biking to visit friends, or helping with physical jobs around the house or yard are all good ways to get active.

FEEL-GOOD FACTOR

Exercise is meant to be fun! Use it to spend time with family and friends, or as time on your own if you need a break from things. Your body will benefit, but it's a great way to enjoy yourself at the same time.

If you haven't exercised for a while, don't worry. Start gradually and over time you'll find your level of fitness increasing so you can push yourself harder. You don't have to train like a top athlete to enjoy the benefits of improved fitness. Any activity that gets you on the move—even for just a few minutes each day—is better than none at all.

More Important than Ever

In recent years, our world has become less physically demanding. We use cars and buses to get around, improved technology has made our work easier, and entertainment has become less active. You may think exercise is tiring—if you're feeling lethargic, surely relaxing in front of the television is what your body needs. But did you know that exercise actually helps you unlock stores of energy in your body? By giving your body a workout, you'll feel more active and ready for the challenges that each day brings.

After a hard day, you may feel like sitting in front of the television, but exercise can give your energy levels a boost.

On the Move!

To get the best from our bodies, we need to do both aerobic and anaerobic exercise. Aerobic exercise helps to increase fitness, while anaerobic exercise strengthens muscles.

Aerobic Exercise

Aerobic exercise includes the activities that make you flushed and out of breath. They get your heart and lungs working hard to supply your muscles with oxygen (aerobic means "with oxygen"). When you start to run or jog, for example, the muscles in your arms and legs tell your brain that they need more oxygen to produce the energy to move. You begin to breathe faster and more deeply, and your heart rate increases.

Jumping rope is an aerobic exercise that increases your heart rate and strengthens your heart and lungs.

As you breathe in more air, your lungs transfer the oxygen to your blood and your beating heart pumps this oxygen-rich blood around your body. This helps your muscles to work at their full potential. As a strong muscle itself, your heart also needs more oxygen to help it beat faster. Your muscles use the oxygen to break down glucose in your food to release energy.

FEEL-GOOD FACTOR

The World Health Organization recommends that teenagers do 60 minutes of moderate to vigorous activity every day for optimum health. Use this as a fitness goal to work toward!

Fighting Fit

The term "fitness" describes how much a person can do with their body. Aerobic exercise helps to improve fitness because it strengthens the heart and lungs. As these organs become stronger, they begin to use oxygen more efficiently (see pages 10–13). A strong heart and lungs means your body uses less energy to pump more oxygen to your body's cells. So the more you exercise, the easier you'll find it to stay active without getting tired.

Increased Metabolism

Combining exercise with a varied diet is also a good way to maintain a healthy weight. When aerobic exercise increases the amount of oxygen in your blood, it helps to burn more energy (calories). This means that fewer unused calories are turned to fat. When you work even harder, your body begins to burn fat as well.

Your body is constantly burning energy to keep going—whether you are active or at rest. These chemical reactions, called your metabolism, help your body to stay fit and healthy. Some people have a naturally fast metabolism, but a combination of aerobic and anaerobic exercise can help to raise your metabolic rate. Muscles burn more calories to maintain themselves than any other tissue in the body. Someone who has a more muscular body through regular exercise, for example, will burn more calories even when they are resting. A higher metabolic rate is good for maintaining a healthy weight, but it also helps release energy, giving you extra vitality.

It's Only Natural

Exercise is something that our bodies are designed to do. Did you know that it's easier to walk for 30 minutes than to stand still for

DID YOU KNOW?

Compared to apes, the human body is well designed for running. Humans have longer legs (for a full stride), ligaments that help to keep the head steady while running, narrower waists so the upper body rotates as the legs move, enlarged semi-circular canals in the ears to aid balance, shorter toes for stability, and large buttock muscles to counteract the forward lean of a running pose.

30 minutes? Studies have also shown that the exercising habits of our ancestors helped to influence the body's development. Our ancestors used running as a survival technique—as hunters and gatherers, they would look for vultures circling above a carcass, and run long distances to reach it before other scavengers got there.

When you exercise, your body burns the energy from the food you eat.

On the Move!

The Aerobic System

Your heart, lungs, and blood are called your aerobic system. Together, they use oxygen from the air you breathe to help unlock the energy your body needs to get active. Your heart is the strongest muscle in your body. It constantly beats but never gets tired. Your heart pumps oxygen-rich blood to your body's cells. When you exercise, your muscles need even more oxygen, so your heart has to work harder.

Heart to Heart

Your heart is just behind your breastbone, slightly to the left of the middle of your chest. It has four chambers—two ventricles and two atria. When your heart beats, the atria contract and push blood into the ventricles. When the ventricles contract, blood is pushed out of the heart. The muscles then relax, and the heart chambers fill with blood again.

The right side of the heart pumps blood to the lungs to pick up oxygen (see page 12). The left side pumps oxygen-rich blood around the body. This blood travels to the cells, tissues, and organs through a network of blood vessels called arteries. Your cells use the oxygen in your blood to release energy from the food you eat. At the same time, they replace the oxygen with carbon dioxide—a waste product of this process. The blood then travels back to the heart through a network of veins.

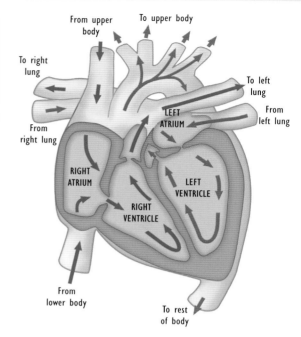

Your heart is a hard-working organ—blood travels through it more than 1,000 times a day.

Body Processes

A strong heart can help other body processes, too. When your heart works efficiently, the blood flow helps to maintain a healthy body temperature. Poor blood circulation, for example, can cause the hands and feet to get cold very easily. As we get older, regular exercise can also help to prevent a narrowing or loss of small blood vessels around the body.

When you exercise, you get hot because your body is burning energy. Your skin also feels flushed. This is because your blood vessels widen to carry blood to the skin's surface, to let the heat escape. This widening of the blood vessels is good for your health. When blood flows more freely through the arteries, fatty deposits and blood clots are less likely to build up and cause illnesses such as heart disease. A widening of the arteries can also prevent, delay, or reduce the symptoms of high blood pressure.

DID YOU KNOW?

When you're resting, your heart pumps about 1.3 gallons (5 L) of blood around your body every minute. When you exercise, this can increase to about 6.6 gallons (25 L) a minute.

FEEL-GOOD FACTOR

There are many ways to get active. Try biking, running, brisk walking, or a group activity. Taking the stairs instead of the escalator and running to the bus stop are a good start! Build up your fitness gradually and soon you'll be on the road to a new, improved you.

You get flushed during exercise because your blood vessels widen to carry blood to the surface of your skin.

Target Zone

To get the most out of aerobic activity, you need to feel your heart beat rapidly. This means doing exercises that increase your heart rate to between 50 and 75 percent of your maximum heart rate (your maximum heart rate is 220 beats per minute, minus your age). This range is called your "target zone" (see page 26).

If you haven't exercised for a while, aim for the lower part of this range for the first few months. Start with a brisk walk or jog for just 5, 10, or 15 minutes. Over time, you'll find that you can gradually work harder to raise your heart rate. It's important to exercise at a pace that's right for you. You should be able to talk while you work out. If you can't, you are exercising too hard—slow down and let your body recover.

If you haven't exercised for a while, try gentle jogging to begin with—or even a brisk walk!

On the Move!

Take a Deep Breath

Your lungs are the key to the oxygen that keeps your body going. When you breathe in, your lungs help to transfer oxygen from the air to your bloodstream. When you exercise, you breathe even more deeply to supply the extra oxygen that your body needs. The amount of air your lungs can hold is called your lung capacity. The average human can hold about 1.6 gallons (6 L) of air in their lungs, but only a small amount of this is used when you breathe.

The amount of air that you breathe in depends on your activity. When you're resting, you take about 15 breaths a minute, taking in about 3 gallons (12 L) of air. From this, your lungs absorb about 1/2 pint of oxygen. Most people double their air intake when they exercise. When some top athletes exercise, however, they breathe in much more air. This increases their breathing rate to 40 gallons (150 L) of air (about 1.3 gallons (5 L) of oxygen) a minute.

Gas Exchange

Every time you take a breath, the air travels down a series of tubes from your windpipe into your lungs. The tubes divide into smaller branches called bronchi until they become tiny air sacs called alveoli. The alveoli are covered with small blood vessels called capillaries. With each breath, the alveoli fill with air and the capillaries absorb the oxygen into your blood. This oxygen-rich blood travels to your heart and is then transferred to the rest of your body to be used by your cells.

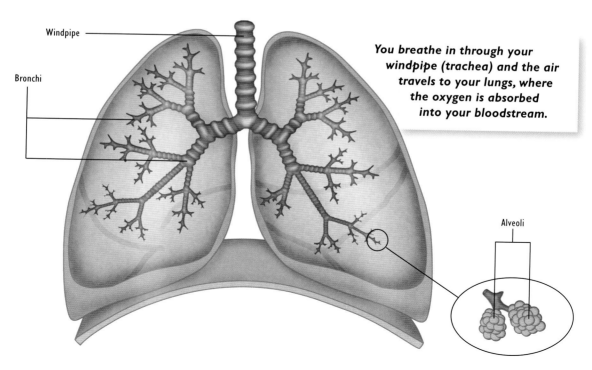

Windpipe

Bronchi

Alveoli

You breathe in through your windpipe (trachea) and the air travels to your lungs, where the oxygen is absorbed into your bloodstream.

The right side of the heart pumps oxygen-poor blood to the lungs—to pick up oxygen and to release carbon dioxide (see page 10). Oxygen-rich blood then returns to the left side of the heart, where it is pumped to the rest of the body. This is why the air you breathe in is rich in oxygen, while the air you breathe out is rich in carbon dioxide.

Strengthening Your Lungs

Regular exercise will help to strengthen the muscles in your chest and increase your lung capacity. Your lungs won't actually change in size, but they'll become more flexible and able to take in more air. They'll also become better at extracting oxygen from the air you breathe and expelling carbon dioxide. This means you'll be less likely to get out of breath when you exercise. Strong lungs reduce the strain on your heart, too, giving your heart less work to do to supply your muscles with oxygen. Try to breathe deeply when you exercise to strengthen your heart and lungs.

A peak flow meter monitors lung capacity by measuring the rate at which air is expelled from your lungs.

Build Your Strength

Anaerobic exercise involves short bursts of intense activity followed by periods of rest. Examples include sprinting or weight-lifting. Anaerobic exercise helps to strengthen your muscles.

Energy Supply

While aerobic exercise gets more oxygen into your bloodstream, during anaerobic exercise your body uses up oxygen faster than your lungs can supply it. Anaerobic means "without (or with little) oxygen." Anaerobic exercise helps you to build stronger, more flexible muscles (see pages 16–17) and improves stamina.

During aerobic exercise, your heart and lungs work hard to get oxygen to your muscles to release energy. This process can take a couple of minutes to get working. In contrast, in anaerobic exercise, your muscles need to access quick bursts of energy right away. If there is not enough oxygen to do this, the body uses chemical sources of fuel or stored glucose in the body. Your body can only perform without oxygen for a limited time. This is why you should alternate short bursts of anaerobic activity with periods of rest.

Lifting weights is an anaerobic activity that improves stamina and muscle flexibility.

Anaerobic exercise helps to improve your general fitness, but in particular your speed and stamina. This will enable you to inject bursts of energy into your activities. If you want to be able to sprint for the bus or sprint on the field, anaerobic training will help you reach your goals.

Lactic Acid

When you exercise, your muscles produce lactic acid. When you exercise hard, for example by sprinting, the levels of lactic acid increase. Sometimes, it can be difficult for your body to remove the lactic acid from your muscles quickly. If the lactic acid levels get too high, a reaction with other body chemicals can cause lactic acid to build up in the muscles. This makes your muscles feel tired or tender when you overwork.

DID YOU KNOW?

Anaerobic exercise doesn't burn fat (your body needs oxygen to do that). However, by strengthening muscles, it speeds up your metabolic rate so you continue to burn fat after you exercise.

In small doses, lactic acid doesn't damage your body. In fact, the pain is useful because it tells you to stop working your body too hard. As you slow down, your body is able to recover and increase oxygen levels again to flush away the lactic acid. Too much lactic acid can be harmful, however. Giving your body a chance to recover between exercises helps to reduce the levels of lactic acid in your bloodstream.

A quick sprint to catch the bus gives you a burst of anaerobic activity!

Regular aerobic and anaerobic exercise can actually help your body become more efficient at removing lactic acid from your muscles. If you strengthen and build your muscles, and increase oxygen levels through improved lung capacity, your body will be able to cope with higher levels of lactic acid.

Interval Training

Interval training is a particularly good way to enjoy an anaerobic workout. By alternating anaerobic exercises (short sprints or lifting weights) with periods of rest or aerobic activity, you allow your body to recover before pushing it hard again. If you already have a basic level of fitness, try walking for a minute, jogging or sprinting for 10 seconds, and then walking for a minute again. Repeating this process will help train your body to access stored energy in short, sharp bursts. Increasing your muscle strength and endurance will also help you to make muscle movements more quickly.

REAL LIFE

"I love playing on the soccer team, but by halftime I'm really tired. In the second half, it can be difficult to find the energy to sprint for the ball. My coach recommended interval training, to improve my fitness and to build my speed." Matt, 14

Build Your Strength

Body Conditioning

As well as helping to condition your heart and lungs, exercise is good for muscles and bones. Exercise helps to build, maintain, and strengthen bones, joints, and muscles, reducing the risk of breaks and strains. A good workout also increases the flexibility and range of movement in the joints.

Muscle Power

You have more than 600 skeletal muscles in your body that move and support your bones or help with delicate movements such as blinking. Some skeletal muscles are attached to your bone joints by a flexible cord or sheet called a tendon. These skeletal muscles contract and relax to help your bones move. When two bones meet at a joint, tissues called ligaments fasten the bones together, stabilizing the joint.

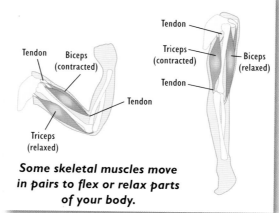

Some skeletal muscles move in pairs to flex or relax parts of your body.

Skeletal muscles are made of bundles of long, thin fibers called myocytes that overlap when a muscle contracts, and stretch out when a muscle relaxes. These muscle fibers contain filaments (strands) of actin or myosin proteins. Thick myosin fibers give you strength in short bursts—if you need to lift a heavy weight, for example. These fibers are sometimes called "fast twitch" fibers. They are good for anaerobic exercise, when you need a sudden burst of strength or speed. Thinner actin fibers (or "slow twitch" fibers) are good for aerobic exercise, when you need to work for a longer period of time. They use oxygen in your blood to release energy. These are the fibers you use if you want to run a marathon, or cycle or swim long distances.

Push-ups strengthen the muscles in the chest and shoulders.

Stay in Shape

Your muscles need to be exercised regularly to keep them firm and strong. People who are hospitalized for a long period of time, or are confined to bed rest, find that their muscles weaken through lack of use. Weak muscles can affect your appearance—without exercise, muscles begin to shrink, changing your body's shape. Weak muscles can affect your posture because there is less support for your skeleton and joints. Weak stomach muscles can also change the position of the organs inside your body.

Building Muscles

To grow and strengthen your muscles, you need to do some form of resistance (or strength) training. This means working your muscles hard for a short period of time. Anaerobic exercises help to increase the number of filaments in your muscle fibers—the fibers literally grow to cope with the extra demands placed on them. During anaerobic exercise, the fast twitch fibers grow faster and larger than the slow twitch fibers, giving you stronger, denser muscles. Because these muscle fibers burn a lot of energy, they will also help your body to burn fat. Muscles store energy in the form of glucose, too. This means that larger, stronger muscles increase your ability to store energy.

You can strengthen almost any muscle group in the body by doing different exercises. Push-ups are a simple way to strengthen your chest, arm, and shoulder muscles, for example. You can work other muscle groups using light weights. Do a few repetitive movements followed by a period of rest. In a matter of weeks, you can begin to increase the amount of weight you are lifting as you get stronger. Some activites are particularly good for building muscles. Horse riding strengthens the muscles in your legs, buttocks, and back, for example.

Canoeing or kayaking trains your upper arm and back muscles, and rowing uses your back and leg muscles.

Build Your Strength

Keeping Strong

Like muscles, your bones have a "use it or lose it" quality. Just as muscles grow and strengthen when you place demands on them, bones become stronger and denser when they are used. You probably think your bones are like the skeletons you see in a museum, but they are actually living tissues that constantly grow and repair themselves. Like muscles, your bones respond to the stresses and strains of everyday life.

Studies have shown that on average, astronauts in space lose two percent of their bone mass a month (whereas people usually lose two percent a decade after the age of 35). The lack of gravity in space means that bones don't have to support the body for movement or posture. Without everyday stresses and strains, the skeleton begins to shrink. Most astronauts experience bone loss in the lower half of their bodies—the weight-bearing leg bones, for example, that are no longer used. Astronauts now use special equipment in space, with springs, elastic, and vacuum pumps to keep up their resistance training and prevent muscle loss.

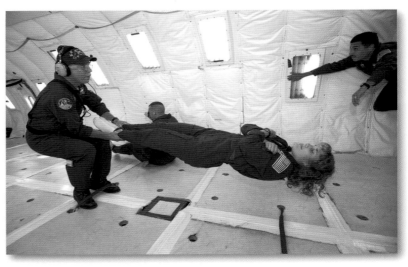

Astronauts have to train hard to keep up their muscle strength in zero-gravity conditions.

GOOD VIBRATIONS

Scientists have found that it is not just large stresses or strains on your bones that keep them growing. Small muscle twitches during everyday activities such as standing or walking have been found to affect bones. To keep your body upright, groups of muscle cells rapidly twitch. This is the slight trembling you can feel if you squat and rest your hands on your thighs.

Growing Bones

When you exercise, you're telling your bone-building cells to get to work. Weight-bearing exercises (when your bones and muscles work against gravity) are particularly good for your skeleton. These include aerobics, dancing, walking, jogging, climbing stairs, and lifting weights. Activities that put your bones under the stress of movement and the pull of your muscles encourage them to build more cells and become stronger. Improving and maintaining the density of your bones can also prevent serious diseases later in life such as osteoporosis, which causes the bones to weaken and break more easily.

This is especially important when you're a teenager because your bones and joints are still growing. Most bone growth happens between 10 and 16 years of age, with bone mass reaching a peak between the ages of 20 and 30. In adolescence, regular exercise can increase bone density by as much as 2–8 percent a year. Studies have also shown that exercise as a teenager can improve bone density later in life. Women, for example, usually gain 40–50 percent of their bone mass during adolescence. Scientists have found that women who exercised regularly during those years had a higher hip-bone density later in life than those who did not.

Staying Flexible

Your bones are too strong to bend, but your joints, and the muscles attached to them, allow them to move. Just like the oiled parts of a car, you need to move your joints regularly to keep them flexible. Exercise can actually help to strengthen your joints, too. When you build and tone your muscles, the joints that they support become stronger and firmer. This reduces the risk of injury and, by giving you good posture, helps to avoid problems of joint or back pain later in life.

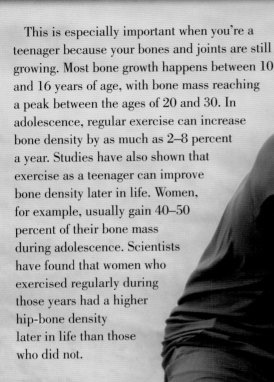

DID YOU KNOW?

Some professional tennis players have 35 percent more bone in their playing arm. Scientists believe this bone growth is caused by signals sent out by contracting muscles.

Brain Power

As well as giving your body a good workout, exercise is also beneficial to your brain. Studies have shown that physical activity can even build brain cells and improve your memory.

New Cells

When you exercise, you increase the flow of oxygen and blood to your organs, including your brain. Studies have shown that a workout can actually improve the function of the brain, helping with school work, memory, and concentration. Exercise has been found to help generate new brain cells (neurons) in the hippocampus, the area of the brain used for learning and memory. Increased oxygen and blood flow to the brain also repairs and protects existing neurons. Scientists believe that the mild stress caused by physical activity encourages these neurons to grow, in a process called neurogenesis.

Studies have shown that the memory-enhancing effects of exercise are most obvious in aging brains, where there is room for improvement and the changes are clearly seen. Exercise is thought to be particularly beneficial for patients with diseases such as Alzheimer's and Parkinson's, which are caused by a loss of neurons. People in the early stages of Alzheimer's disease have more brain volume in areas that are important to memory when they are physically fit, compared to patients who are less active.

Keeping active through life can help the part of your brain that controls memory.

REAL LIFE

"My gran had Alzheimer's before she died. She got confused easily and I know it frustrated her greatly. I hope I don't have the same disease when I grow old. If exercise helps, it's got to be a good thing."
Susan, 14

A Look Inside

Scientists were unsure exactly why exercise caused neurogenesis, but in 2008, a study at the University of North Carolina found that people who had been exercising regularly for a long period of time had more small blood vessels in their brains and more blood flow than people who were inactive. The growth of new blood vessels —angiogenesis— occurs around the body in response to regular exercise, and this new study showed that the brain is no exception. At the moment, increased brainpower has been linked to aerobic activity, but in the future new studies will look at the effect of anaerobic exercise on brain function, too.

A Head Start

Although studies of neurogenesis have focused on elderly patients, establishing an exercise routine in your teens is a good way to help maintain brain function later in life. At about 30 years of age, the brain starts to lose nerve tissue. Although it was once thought that brainpower diminished as cells died with age, this new research showed that the brain can continue

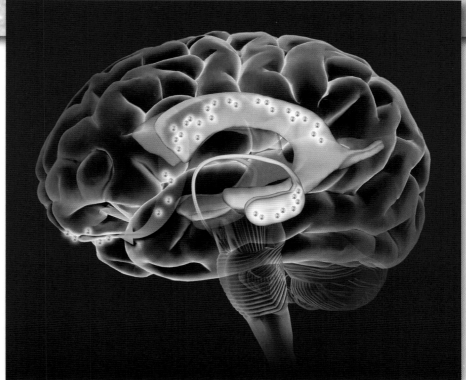

Neurogenesis is the development of new brain cells (neurons). Here, neurons develop in one part of the brain and then travel to another, where they become sensory neurons.

to generate new brain cells as you get older. Aerobic activity helps to reinforce the neuron connections in your brain as you age so that you can continue to process and store information. Don't overdo exercise on account of your brain, however. Unfortunately, it's not possible to exercise to pure brilliance!

GIVE IT A TRY!

Between 6 and 15 years of age, the human brain grows most in the parietal lobes, which affect movement and physical coordination, and the temporal lobes, which affect language abilities. The skills you learn as a child and teenager are "hardwired" in the brain. If you want to learn a new sport, now is the time to try out new skills!

Brain Power

Exercise releases endorphins in your brain—these are the chemicals that make you feel happy!

REAL LIFE

"It was exam time and I was feeling really stressed. Mom said I should go out and get some fresh air, but I had too much work to do. Then Chris called and suggested soccer in the park. Just an hour's game really helped to clear my head, and I had the best night's sleep in ages."
David, 15

Happy Times

While we may not be able to exercise to intellectual heights, there are no limits to the ways that exercise can make us feel good. Vigorous exercise, such as swimming, running, or cycling, releases endorphins that encourage feelings of happiness. These hormones are usually released by the pituitary gland in the brain in response to stress or pain. They help to minimize any aches and pains that you might feel when you exercise and can produce a feeling of euphoria. Endorphins usually start to take effect after about 30 minutes of physical activity.

For people who exercise vigorously on a regular basis, the release of endorphins can have an addictive effect: the more you exercise, the more you need to do to achieve the same level of euphoria. But unlike some addictions—such as drinking or drugs—the 30-minute delay in endorphin release means that few people get truly addicted to exercise. It's important, however, not to allow exercise to become an obsession.

Relieving Depression

Exercise can also help relieve symptoms of depression and anxiety. Studies have shown that people who are physically active recover more quickly from bouts of mild depression.

The increased blood flow caused by exercise can help to flush away waste products from the brain that build up when you're stressed or working hard.

Regular exercise can also protect mental health as we age because it increases levels of natural antidepressants in the brain, such as serotonin and norepinephrine. Scientists have also found that depression can be alleviated by neurogenesis (see page 20). In depressed women, for example, the brain's hippocampus has been found to be up to 15 percent smaller than usual.

Relaxing Your Mind

Whatever the brain-boosting benefits of exercise, it's certain that a workout in the fresh air will help to relax and ease your mind. This is especially important if you're working your brain extra hard—with exams or coursework, for example. By improving blood flow to the brain, exercise brings more oxygen and nutrients that help you to think clearly. By helping to release endorphins into the bloodstream, exercise can make you feel more positive and better able to cope with stressful situations. It will also help you to get a good night's rest—a healthy body, with tired muscles, finds it easier to relax and sleep.

FEEL-GOOD FACTOR

A relaxed mind is good for your circulatory system. Stress and tension can cause your blood vessels to deteriorate as you get older and can raise your blood pressure. Taking action to keep stress levels down is a sure way to a healthier you.

Improving Fitness

Regular exercise affects how well your heart, lungs, muscles, and brain work, but it also affects how long you can keep going (your stamina) and how flexible (limber) your body is.

Olympic marathon runners like Samuel Kamau Wanjiru train for years to build up their stamina for the long race.

Increased Stamina

When you exercise, your body uses energy to keep itself going. If you have stamina, you can run a long way without getting out of breath. Stamina isn't something that you either have or don't have. It's something you can work at to build up gradually.

To improve your stamina, you need to train your body to become more efficient so it uses less energy when you move around. The best way to improve your stamina is to strengthen your heart and lungs through aerobic activity. Making your heart work harder can thicken the heart muscle, giving it more power to push out blood. A strong heart can squirt out more blood with each heartbeat, so it can beat less while you do the same

FEEL-GOOD FACTOR

Jumping rope is one of the most effective exercises for boosting levels of stamina. Believe it or not, 10 minutes of jumping rope requires about the same effort as a 30-minute run. You could even learn new tricks with a jump rope to liven up your stamina training.

amount of exercise with less effort. In the same way, if you increase your lung capacity (see page 12), your body can absorb more oxygen with fewer breaths. The more exercise you do, the easier it gets.

How Much is Enough?

You need to get your heart rate up when you do aerobic exercise to really improve your fitness. During aerobic exercise, your pulse rate should rise slightly for a sustained period of time (see page 26). Short bursts of intense exercise that make your pulse rate rocket won't be effective for your overall fitness—you'll just feel exhausted and will need to stop.

There are some great physical activities out there to help you to develop stamina—rowing, canoeing, dancing, windsurfing, volleyball,

Aerobic sports such as basketball are great for increasing your stamina and making your body use energy more efficiently.

soccer, basketball, or even housework are just a few examples. Find an activity that you enjoy and build up gradually. Keep an exercise diary of how you find each session. You'll be amazed at how much progress you make in just a few weeks.

Muscle Strength

Strengthening and toning your muscles through anaerobic exercise will also help your body to endure sudden bursts of energy and will give you added strength for everyday tasks. As you increase the muscle fibers in your body, your muscles will store extra energy for when you need it most (see page 17). You'll also train your body to effectively access this stored energy for times when the oxygen supply to your muscles is limited.

Improving Fitness

You can feel your pulse in your wrist.

Measuring Fitness

When you exercise, your heart beats faster. This means that your pulse rate increases, too. The pulse can be felt in places of the body where an artery can be lightly compressed against a bone—in your wrist or your neck, for example. The pressure of blood flowing through the arteries causes a pulse. This is not a measure of the speed at which your blood is flowing—a pulse rate is usually about 10–15 times faster than actual blood flow. Pulse rates vary from person to person and slow down as you get older. As you become fitter, you'll also find that your pulse rate becomes lower, both at rest and when you exercise. This is because your heart has been trained to work less hard at supplying your muscles with oxygen.

Taking Your Pulse

Your pulse rate shows the number of times your heart beats in one minute. To take your pulse, place your index and second finger on the palm side of your wrist, below the base of your thumb. Alternatively, you can place these fingers on your neck, on one side of your windpipe. Press lightly until you feel the blood pulsing below your fingers. You may need to adjust your fingers slightly until you feel the movement. Use a watch with a second hand to count how many pulses you can feel for 10 seconds. Multiply this number by six to get your pulse rate per minute.

To find out if you are exercising in your target zone (see page 11), take a break from your activity and check your 10-second pulse. This will help you to know whether you need to increase or reduce your level of exertion.

If you become out of breath when you exercise, give your body a chance to slow down.

If you find it difficult to take your pulse when you exercise, you can also figure out how effectively you're working by how you feel. You should be slightly out of breath when you exercise, but still be able to talk. If you can't, you've pushed yourself too hard. Slow down until you get your breath back.

Staying Fit

Although your pulse rate drops as you get fitter, a low pulse rate doesn't mean you should stop exercising altogether.

RESTING HEART RATE

Age	Beats per minute
Up to 1	100–160
1–10	60–140
10+	60–100
Athletes	40–60

TARGET HEART RATE DURING EXERCISE

Age	Beats per minute
15	123–164
20	120–160
25	117–156
30	114–152

As your stamina increases, you'll find that you need to do more to keep your pulse rate in the target zone and for your fitness level to rise. Everyone's pulse rate is different, so get used to what works for you. And work to the level of fitness you want to achieve. Not everyone strives to be fit enough to complete a half-marathon—what's more important is that your fitness levels are helping to improve your quality of life.

Stretch and Flex

Keeping on the move is one thing, but if you're strong and supple, too, you'll find that you can do more with your body and move with greater confidence.

Staying Limber

The stretchier your muscles and tendons are, the more limber you are. Staying limber helps you to move your body smoothly and confidently, without jarring. Flexible muscles are also the key to good posture and coordination. Stretching helps to tone muscles throughout your body, and your movements become less restricted as your muscles grow more flexible. More importantly, your flexibility can affect the way that you move when you exercise, making you less likely to suffer from strains, sprains, or stiffness. Tight or stiff muscles put pressure on your joints when you exercise and can lead to an injury.

If you're limber, you find it easy to bend, stretch, and twist into different positions.

Longer Muscles

Stretching is a great way to improve suppleness and flexibility. Your skeletal muscles stretch to a certain length when you move and contract them. This length is determined by the flexibility of your muscles as well as the flexibility of the tendons and ligaments that keep them in place. Stretching can gently encourage the ligaments, tendons, and muscles to lengthen. It also gives room for the blood vessels to expand, helping to increase the blood flow through your body.

Warming Up

It's good to stretch before and after you exercise. Stretching after a light warm-up will improve the flexibility of your joints and muscles, and make you less likely to experience strains and sprains (see page 34). After exercise, stretching can relieve any tightness in your muscles and help the body to recover as you cool down. You'll find it easier to stretch after you've been active. This is because blood flow has increased and your body has warmed up.

Whatever type of exercise you decide to do, it is important to stretch before you begin.

By doing gentle exercises, you can gradually stretch the tissues around your muscles to make your muscles and tendons longer and stronger. But remember, everyone is different—some people have longer, looser muscles than others. You may find it difficult to touch your toes, while your friend can put her fingertips on the floor. That's okay! Don't stretch yourself beyond what feels comfortable for you.

Stretch and Flex

Take a Break

Stretching can be done at any time of day, and it's a great way to relax and de-stress. Your muscles work hard throughout the day, even when you're standing or sitting still. Taking time out to stretch your muscles helps increase the blood flow around your body and gives your muscles a breather.

During your teenage years, you spend a lot of time sitting in school and in front of a computer. It's hard to remember to stretch, but you can do lots of simple exercises, even when sitting down. Now is the time to develop a good posture to avoid joint and back pain when you get older, and to keep your joints strong.

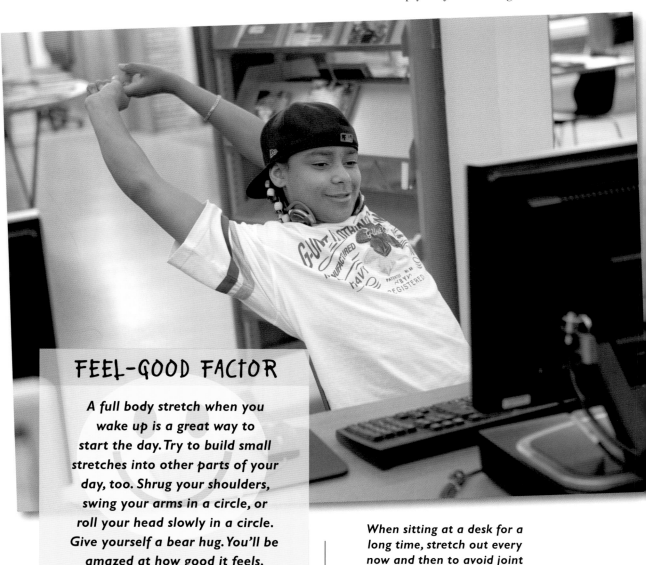

FEEL-GOOD FACTOR

A full body stretch when you wake up is a great way to start the day. Try to build small stretches into other parts of your day, too. Shrug your shoulders, swing your arms in a circle, or roll your head slowly in a circle. Give yourself a bear hug. You'll be amazed at how good it feels.

When sitting at a desk for a long time, stretch out every now and then to avoid joint and back pain.

Stretching Exercises

Try these simple stretching exercises to improve your flexibility. Stretch slowly and gently, without sudden movements or jerks that could pull or strain a muscle. Don't bounce when you stretch—this can strain your muscles before they are properly warmed up. If you include gentle stretching as part of your exercise routine, in a few weeks you'll find that you're able to move and stretch more than ever before.

Front thigh muscles

Kneel on your left knee and put your right foot on the floor in front of you. With your hands on your right knee, slowly raise up your left knee. Hold for five seconds. Repeat three times on each side.

Front thigh muscles and buttocks

Hold on to a chair or lean your right hand against a wall. Bend your left leg up behind you and hold your left foot gently with your left hand. Hold for five seconds. Repeat three times on each side.

Hamstring (back leg) muscles

Balance yourself and put one leg carefully on a low stool or chair. Straighten this leg. Bend the other knee gently to stretch your hamstring. Repeat three times on each side.

Bottom muscles

Lie on your back with your legs bent. Bring one knee up and gently pull it towards your chest. Hold for five seconds. Repeat three times on each side.

Stretch and Flex

Keep Up Your Strength

How strong you are depends on the amount of force that your muscles can produce. The stronger you are, the easier you'll find it to lift or move a heavy weight for a short period of time. If you have endurance, too, you'll be able to lift or move lighter weights repeatedly for longer periods.

Building Strength

To make yourself stronger, you can train particular muscles (or muscle groups) that you use in everyday life. Strengthening your leg muscles will help you to walk or run up hills or stairs. Strengthening your arm and shoulder muscles will help you to lift heavy books or shopping bags. Strengthening exercises help to increase the size of your muscle fibers (see page 17), and if you exercise regularly, you'll maintain this strength for longer.

Strengthening exercises don't just benefit your muscles. As you train, you'll be strengthening your bones and the tendons that keep your joints stable. You'll improve your posture, and you'll find that your stamina increases, too.

Using weights is a good way to give an added boost to your exercise regime.

Weight Training

If you want to try some anaerobic exercise to increase your muscles, lifting light weights will help get you started. You need to do enough repetitions so your muscles feel tired. Always use a weight that feels comfortable to lift. A can of soup is often a good starting point!

REAL LIFE

"I went on the school ski trip last year. We were given exercises to help strengthen our leg muscles. It was hard work at first, but after a week or so they began to get easier. When I got back, I also found I could bike a bit faster to Sam's house!"
Joe, 15

As you increase your strength gradually, you'll find that you can move on to slightly heavier loads. Ideally, the weight should be heavy enough for your muscles to tire in less than 12 repetitions, but light enough that you can do at least 4 repetitions. Remember to rest between repetitions and have at least one day off between working the same muscle groups, to give your muscles a chance to recover.

Where's the Limit?

Don't be disheartened if you find that your progress levels out. Scientists believe that there are limits to the strength, speed, or jumping height that even the top athletes can achieve. Since the first modern Olympics in 1896, athletes have been increasing their speed, year after year. In 1896, for example, the men's 100-meter gold medallist, Tom Burke, ran at a speed of 18.6 mph (30 km/h). In 2009, Usain Bolt ran at more than 23 mph (37 km/h)!

However, scientists believe that this continued increase can't last forever. The biological functions of organs such as the lungs have limited potential. With that said, with improved sports equipment, such as running suits and shoes, improved diets, and coaching techniques, we may well see more records broken.

Usain Bolt has been nicknamed "Lightning Bolt" because of his incredible speed at sprinting.

DID YOU KNOW?

The strongest muscle in the body (based on weight) is the masseter muscle, located in the jaw. It can clench the teeth with a force of up to 55 lbs (25 kg) on the incisors, or 200 lbs (91 kg) on the molars.

Staying Safe

Exercise is meant to be fun, so it's important that you stay safe when you get active to enjoy your workout as much as possible.

Warming Up

One of the most important things to do before you get active is to warm up. Warming up raises your heart rate so you can start to get extra oxygen-rich blood to your muscles. As your body gets warmer, your muscles become more flexible and your joints become more mobile. Stretching and loosening your muscles, limbs, and joints (see page 31) will get your body ready for action and reduce your risk of injury. You should begin exercising at a medium pace to give your body a chance to adjust to the new movements. After about five minutes, you should be warm enough to push yourself harder.

Cooling Down

After you exercise, cooling down will help your body to recover and enable your breathing and heart rate to return to normal. Slow down your movements gradually until you are still—by changing from running to brisk walking, for example. If you stop right away, you may feel dizzy. Stopping gradually also gives your body time to remove lactic acid from your muscles (see page 15).

You may have seen marathon runners wrapped in foil blankets after a race. This ensures that they don't lose their body heat too quickly.

Bend and stretch a little to relax your muscles. This will help to keep your joints supple and will prevent any symptoms of stiffness the next day. Exercise makes you hot, so be careful not to cool down too quickly. Put an extra layer of clothing on when you cool down to avoid getting too chilly.

Know Your Limits

Listen to your body when you exercise. If you feel faint, dizzy, or out of breath, it's a sign that you need to take a break! Slow down and let your body recover. Think about how you want exercise to work for you. Perhaps your goals are to improve your aerobic stamina or to tone your muscles, or a little of both. Even top athletes can't do everything. The chances are that a marathon runner can't lift heavy weights, and a shot-putter can't run long distances. Keep your activities fun and your goals realistic.

Over-exercising, especially if you're tired, can lead to strains and sprains, or more serious injuries. Take a break if you feel you've pushed yourself too hard!

Keeping Safe

Safety First

You don't need expensive equipment to get active, but you should wear suitable clothes and shoes. On cold days, try to wear layers of clothing to keep you warm. Clothes that are loose fitting (but not too baggy) will help you move around comfortably. Materials that absorb sweat, such as cotton, are better than synthetic materials that can make you feel hot. Choose well-fitting shoes that give your foot and ankle adequate support. Tie your shoelaces securely to avoid tripping over them.

If you do use equipment, such as gymnastics apparatus or heavy weights, it's important to have adult supervision. Instructions and guidelines are designed to help you avoid injury. Make sure that you warm up well before you get active. If your body is cold, you'll need more energy to warm up so you'll get tired more easily. Less blood travels to cold muscles, which makes them more prone to injury.

Fuel and Liquids

Try not to exercise after you've just eaten. When your body is digesting, your bloodstream is busy helping your stomach break down and absorb your food. This means your muscles will have less blood flowing to them and will be unable to work at their full potential. Exercising too soon after a meal can also make you feel sick or faint. Try to avoid strenuous exercise for at least two hours after you've eaten. If you exercise first, it's better to take about 20 minutes before having a meal.

It's important to take in fluids both during and after exercise. When you exercise, you lose water as you sweat, so you need to drink more to replace it. Water is essential for your body's cells to function effectively.

Try to drink continually while exercising, rather than all at once.

Where and When?

Exercising outdoors in the fresh air is the best way to give your body the oxygen it needs. But be careful on very hot days in summer. You may prefer to exercise in the morning or the evening when the sun is less severe. If you have severe allergies, exercise in the morning when the pollen count is lower. If you live in a city and like to jog, the morning may also be better, before smoke and fumes fill the air.

In the evening, make sure you wear light or reflective clothing when it gets dark and face oncoming traffic if you jog on the road. Try to jog on soft ground (rather than concrete). Hard surfaces can strain and damage your joints.

FEELING FRESH

Studies have shown that exercising in the fresh air helps to increase alertness and raise your spirits. Outdoor exercise can also burn more energy, especially when it's chilly. Your body uses up to 50 percent more calories just to keep warm. Running on uneven and unfamiliar ground also tones more muscles than an indoor surface.

Exercising outside, such as doing tai chi, increases your oxygen intake and helps keep you alert.

Aches and Pains

Most injuries happen when you're tired, so learn to know when you've done enough. Try to work at improving your stamina so you get less tired when you exercise. Don't be too ambitious— you're more prone to injure yourself if you push yourself too hard. Do what feels right for you.

A good technique is also important to avoid straining or over-stretching. Work at improving your skills and your coordination before you push your body too hard. This will help reduce your risk of injury and will make your exercise routine more effective.

Strains and Sprains

You can pull or tear a muscle if it contracts strongly and the opposite muscle doesn't relax quickly enough. Warming up before you exercise and keeping your body limber will help to prevent these stresses and strains. If you feel a sharp pain when you exercise, stop at once. A hot, relaxing bath can help most minor muscle strains. If a pain continues, however, seek advice from your doctor.

Strains and sprains should be properly supported before continuing exercise.

DID YOU KNOW?

If you strain a muscle, you should rest it for three to five days. During this time, your body produces chemicals and cells to help remove dead muscle fibers and begin the repair process.

Cramp

You've probably experienced a cramp at some time in your life. A cramp is a sharp pain caused by a muscle (or group of muscles) going into spasm, which means they contract but don't relax again. A cramp can occur if your body is in an awkward position, or if you work your body too hard. Cramps can also be caused by a lack of nutrients and fluid in muscle fibers. Warming up properly, eating a good, balanced diet, and drinking small amounts of fluid while you exercise is usually enough to avoid cramps. If you do get a cramp, however, gently stretch, rub, and massage the affected area to relieve the symptoms.

Professional sportsmen and women put their muscles under great pressure when they compete.

Stitches

A stitch is a sudden sharp pain in your side, just under your ribs. It may cause you to slow down or stop exercising altogether. Warming up and not eating too close to physical activity reduces the risk of getting a stitch. There are a number of theories about why a stitch develops. When you exercise, blood moves away from the diaphragm—the muscle that separates the stomach and abdomen from the heart and lungs. This is thought to weaken the diaphragm, causing it to cramp. Other theories point to food and fluids that are slow to digest, causing the stomach to "tug" on the ligaments connected to the diaphragm.

If you get a stitch, slow down or stop and bend forward. Breathing deeply while pressing gently on the painful area can also help to relieve symptoms.

SOCCER FOCUS

In a survey of injuries at a professional soccer club, nearly 27 percent of all injuries involved muscles and tendons. The body's muscles and tendons have to produce large forces for sprinting, jumping, shooting, and heading the ball.

Exercise for Life

To stay fit and healthy, try to make exercise a regular part of your routine. The more activity you build into your day, the better your body will feel and function.

Good Timing

Find a routine that works for you. We all have busy lives and it can be difficult to find time for all the things we want to do. Choose a good time of day. Some people are more alert in the mornings and like to start their day with a burst of energy. Others prefer to wait until later in the day. Some people find that exercising in the evening relaxes their body

FEEL-GOOD FACTOR

Regular activity can help you to feel, look, and work better. Exercise also helps you to learn about yourself, your abilities, your potential, and your limitations. It gives you confidence in yourself and helps you to work with others. There's no doubt that getting active is the first step to enjoying a fuller life.

and helps them to sleep more deeply. Others find that exercising too close to bedtime makes it harder to fall asleep because their mind is racing.

If you often feel tired, remember that improving fitness will help your body to access more energy. Regular activity will help to reduce this fatigue and make you feel more alert each day.

Just taking the dogs for a walk is good exercise and a good habit to get into.

A Regular Routine

Once you've identified the times that are best for you, try to make activities a part of your regular routine. If you get used to a weekly workout, you'll find it easier to keep up your fitness goals and exercise will feel less like a chore. Choose activities you like—that way you'll be more likely to do them regularly and enjoy the benefits that they bring. Remember that exercise can be spread over the week. Sometimes you may only manage 10–15 minutes. The important thing is to make physical activity a regular goal.

It only takes a few minutes a day to become more physically active. For a start, you could run up the stairs or take a brisk walk to the post office. To condition your heart and lungs, up to an hour of regular exercise, three or four times a week is recommended. But if time is an issue, don't let that stop you. Try to find two 15-minute periods or even three 10-minute periods a day. Once you realize how enjoyable a workout can be, you may want to make it a habit! This way, exercise becomes a part of your life without you even realizing it.

A LONGER LIFE

Scientists have discovered that a good daily workout can add four years to your life. In a U.S. study, people who exercised moderately (such as walking for 30 minutes a day, five days a week) lived up to 1.5 years longer than those who were less active. Those who did more vigorous activity (such as running for the equivalent time) lived nearly four years longer.

Joining a gym or taking a class can help you make exercise a part of your weekly routine.

Skateboarding, pilates, or just kicking a ball in the park are all good ways to spend your time and get fit.

Good to Be Young

Studies have shown that teenagers who exercise regularly are more likely to make exercise a lifelong habit. It's never too late to start! Exercise will improve your life now, but you will also feel the benefits in the years ahead. Regular exercise as a teenager can also reduce the risk of illnesses later in life, such as heart disease, high blood pressure, osteoporosis, obesity, arthritis, and cancer.

As you get older, your body changes. Your muscles weaken, your joints become less flexible, and some of your muscle tissue is replaced by fat. Regular exercise when you're young helps you to stay fit through these changing years.

FEEL-GOOD FACTOR

You don't have to be athletic to exercise. Most physical activities can be done without special skills. Walking is a perfect example! Whatever your ability, today is the perfect time to get active for a healthier, happier life.

Keeping at It

Many teenagers stop doing organized sports as they get older. Once you leave school, physical education classes become a thing of the past and it can be difficult to branch out on your own. Unless you like jogging, or you find a group activity that doesn't cost too much, it can be difficult to know where to start. But remember all the health benefits that an active lifestyle brings.

Choose activities that are right for you. You don't have to be sporty to enjoy getting active. Perhaps you'd rather do an exercise DVD at home. You could even start by introducing physical activities into your daily routine—walking to school or your job instead of taking the bus, doing active chores such as gardening at home, or finding a volunteer job that gets you on the move.

If you have specific goals in mind, a variety of activities could help to maximize the benefits of your exercise. Running will help to improve stamina, yoga or dance will aid your flexibility, and resistance training will improve your strength and give you a well-rounded workout. Set your sights on both short- and long-term goals and keep a record of your progress. It will probably inspire you to keep going! Above all, choose activities that you enjoy.

Look Ahead

Look at exercise as a way to do activities with your friends or family and an opportunity to meet new people. Next time you're faced with a challenging walk or an uphill struggle, think about what benefits the activity is having on your body, and over time, just what your body will be able to do for you.

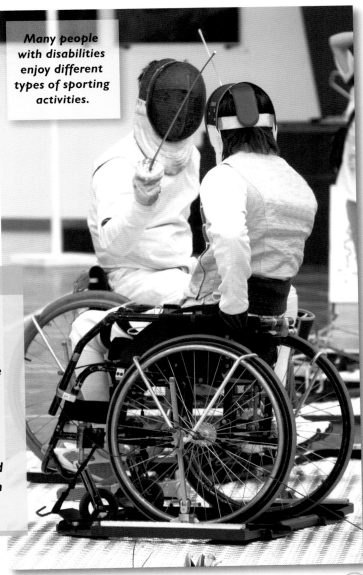

Many people with disabilities enjoy different types of sporting activities.

EXERCISE FOR ALL

If you have a disability, there may be different challenges for you, but it is still important to exercise, and there are plenty of ways to get active. Some amazing athletes have disabilities. Trischa Zorn, a Paralympic swimmer, for example, competed in seven Paralympic Games. Blind since birth, she holds the record for the most gold medals (41) ever won by an athlete in the Olympics or the Paralympics.

Glossary

aerobic exercise any type of exercise that makes the heart and lungs work harder, pumping oxygen-rich blood to the muscles.

Alzheimer's disease a disease of the brain that causes dementia.

anaerobic exercise strenuous exercise that makes the muscles use energy without oxygen.

angiogenesis the formation of new blood vessels in the body.

arteries blood vessels that carry oxygen-rich blood from the heart to the cells, tissues, and organs of the body.

blood pressure the force that blood exerts on the walls of the blood vessels. Blood pressure can vary according to age and general health.

blood vessel a vein, artery, or capillary that carries blood around the body.

calorie a unit for measuring the amount of energy in food. One calorie is the amount of energy needed to raise the temperature of one gram of water by 1°C.

cancer a disease caused by a growth or tumor resulting from an abnormal and uncontrolled division of body cells.

diabetes an illness in which the level of glucose (sugar) in the blood is not properly controlled by the body.

diaphragm the large, flat muscle attached to the bottom of your rib cage that moves to enlarge the chest cavity so your lungs can expand when you breathe in.

endorphins hormones found mainly in the brain that reduce the sensation of pain and produce a feeling of well-being.

endurance the ability to withstand prolonged activity. Also known as stamina.

glucose a type of sugar that your body cells convert into energy.

heart disease a narrowing or blockage of the blood vessels that provide oxygen-rich blood to the heart, caused by a buildup of fatty substances in the blood vessels that restrict blood flow.

heart rate the number of heartbeats per unit of time, usually expressed as beats per minute.

hormones chemical messengers produced by glands in the body. Hormones are transported by the blood to instruct cells and organs to work in a particular way.

immune system a system of organs, tissues, cells, and substances that protect the body against disease and infection.

ligaments fibrous tissues that fasten bones together across a joint.

limber how flexible your body is.

metabolism the chemical reactions that take place in the body to maintain life and to carry out vital processes.

neurogenesis the growth and development of nervous tissue.

obesity when a person has an abnormally high amount of body fat.

osteoporosis a disease that causes the bones to weaken and makes them more prone to breaking.

Parkinson's disease a disease of the nervous system that causes tremors and slow movement.

skeletal muscles muscles that are mostly attached to bones.

tendons the long, stringy fibrous tissues that attach muscles to bones.

veins blood vessels that carry oxygen-poor blood back to the heart.

Further Information

Books

Exercise (It's Your Health!)
By Beverley Goodger
Smart Apple Media, 2006.

Fitness for Fun!
By Dana Meachen Rau
Compass Point Books, 2009.

Food Choices: The Ultimate Teen Guide
By Robin F. Brancato
Scarecrow Press, 2010.

Frequently Asked Questions About Exercise Addiction
By Edward Willett
Rosen Publishing, 2009

Wellbeing (Healthy Habits)
By Jayne Denshire
Smart Apple Media, 2011.

What Happens to Your Body When You Swim? (The How and Why of Exercise)
By Jeanne Nagle
Rosen Central, 2010.

Web Sites

American Heart Association: Fitness
http://www.americanheart.org/presenter. jhtml?identifier=1200013

Center for Disease Control: Obesity Information
http://www.cdc.gov/obesity/

Questions and Answers About Physical Health
http://www.teenhealthfx.com/answers/ Sports/index.php

Teen Exercise
http://www.teensexercise.com/Exercise. html

Teen Health on Fitness and Keeping Healthy
http://www.teenshealth.org

Tone Teen: Exercises for Different Parts of the Body
http://www.toneteen.com

U.S. Government-sponsored Food Safety Information
http://www.foodsafety.gov/

WebMD Information on Aerobic Exercise for Teens
http://www.webmd.com/fitness-exercise/ aerobic-exercise-for-teens

Index